The A to Z Food Joke Book

From **Almond** to **Zucchini**!

Illustrated by Vasco Icuza

Kane Miller
A DIVISION OF EDC PUBLISHING

GIGGLE!
HE HE!
CACKLE!
HA HA!
BWAHAHA!
HAHAHA!
CHORTLE!
LOL!
TEE-HEE!
HAH!

The A to Z Food Joke Book

If you're hungry for hilarious jokes,
and love nothing more than making others laugh,
then this is the perfect book for you!

The A to Z Food Joke Book is a rib-tickling
collection of over 300 food-themed one-liners.
The jokes are ordered alphabetically, so you can
chuckle your way from A to Z, or search for a joke
about your favorite food. From an amusing
almond to zany zucchini, the laughs don't stop!

The A to Z Food Joke Book will really
whet your appetite for joke telling!

Q Why was the **ALMOND** late for work?

A Traffic was nuts!

Q What do you call **ALPHABET SOUP** with only I, V, X, L, C, D, and M?

A Ramen numerals!

Q How many **ANCHOVIES** does it take to change a light bulb?

A Anchovies don't change light bulbs—you're thinking of electric eels!

Q What are cannibals' favorite kinds of **APPETIZERS**?

A Finger foods!

HA HA!

Q What kind of **APPLE** isn't an apple?

A A pineapple!

Q Why can't you make **APPLE COBBLER** with 3.14 apples?

A Because then it would be a pi!

Q What do you call an **APPLE JUICE** without ice?

A Apple ju!

Q What happened when the **APPLE PIE** fell in love with the applesauce?

A They lived apple-ly ever after!

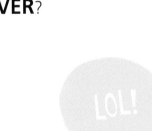

Q How do you make an **APPLE TURNOVER**?

A Push it down a hill!

Q Who led all the **APPLES** to the bakery?

A The Pie Piper!

LOL!

Q Why did the **APRICOT** have a hair transplant?

A It wanted to be a peach!

HAH!

Q What do you call a conversation between two **ARTICHOKES**?

A A heart-to-heart!

Q What do you call a sad **ASPARAGUS**?

A Despair-agus!

Q How did the **AVOCADO** feel after a day at the gym?

A Hard core!

Q What did the tortilla chip say to the **AVOCADO DIP** when it was all gone?

A "We've hit guac bottom!"

Q What do you call a fir tree that grows **BACON**?

A A porky-pine!

Q What do ghosts put on **BAGELS**?

A Scream cheese!

Q How do you tell the difference between a can of soup and a can of **BAKED BEANS**?

A Read the label!

Q What do you call a spinning **BAKED POTATO**?

A A rotate-o!

Q When should you work at a **BAKERY**?

A When you knead some dough!

HAHAHA!

Q What does bread do after **BAKING**?

A Loaf around!

CACKLE!

Q Why do some people eat **BAKING POWDER** when they get up?

A It helps them to rise!

Q What do you call two **BANANA PEELS**?

A A pair of slippers!

Q What type of key opens all **BANANAS**?

A A monkey!

Q Why did the skeleton go to the **BARBECUE**?

A It needed another rib!

Q What is a zombie's favorite type of **BEAN**?

A Human bean!

HE HE!

Q What kinds of **BEANS** can't you grow in a garden?

A Jelly beans!

Q What unit of energy do you get from **BEEF**?

A Cow-lories!

Q What do you call a **BERRY PATCH** on a windy day?

A Blew-berries!

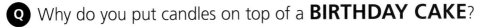

Q Why do you put candles on top of a **BIRTHDAY CAKE**?

A Because it's hard to put them on the bottom!

Q What ingredient do you need to bake dog **BISCUITS**?

A Collie-flour!

Q What did one **BLACKBERRY** say to the other blackberry?

A "If you weren't so sweet, we'd be in a real jam!"

Q Why do **BLOOD ORANGES** help vampires see in the dark?

A They are full of vitamin see!

Q What do you call it when a group of **BLUEBERRIES** play jazz music?

A A jam session!

BWAHAHA!

Q What do you get if you cross a steam train with a **BLUEBERRY PIE**?

A Puff pastry!

B

TEE-HEE!

Q What do you use to carry **BOILED POTATOES**?

A A tater tote!

Q What do you say to someone who ate all your **BRAZIL NUTS**?

A "That's nut-thing to be proud of!"

Q What did the **BREAD** say to the melted cheese?

A "I'm so fondue of you!"

Q What do snowmen eat for **BREAKFAST**?

A Ice krispies!

Q Why did the **BROCCOLI** win the race?

A Because it was a head!

Q What do you get if you spill **BROTH** on a comic book?

A Souper-man!

Q What's another term for **BRUSSELS SPROUTS**?

A Cabbage patch kids!

Q What did the **BURGERS** name their daughter?

A Patty!

CHORTLE!

Q Why can't you trust a **BURRITO**?

A They tend to spill the beans!

Q What did the **BUTTER** say to the bread?

A "I'm on a roll!"

Q Why did the store sell both purple and green **CABBAGES**?

A Because two heads are better than one!

Q What kind of **CAKE** do baseball players like best?

A Bundt cake!

GIGGLE!

Q How do **CANDY BARS** laugh?

A They snicker!

Q Which are the most expensive **CANDY CANES**?

A The ones in mint condition!

Q Why did the **CARROT** win an award?

A Because it was outstanding in its field!

Q What did the **CELERY** say to the hummus?

A "I'm stalking you!"

Q What fruits do ghosts put on their **CEREAL**?

A Boo-nanas and boo-berries!

Q What did the **CHEDDAR CHEESE** say when it was cut into hundreds of pieces?

A "Well, that's just grate!"

Q What do you call **CHEESE** that isn't yours?

A Nacho cheese!

SNICKER!

Q What kind of music do **CHEESEMAKERS** listen to?

A R & Brie!

Q Why are **CHEFS** so mean?

A Because they beat eggs and whip cream!

GUFFAW!

Q Why did the **CHEWING GUM** cross the road?

A It was stuck to the chicken's foot!

Q Why shouldn't you eat plates and plates of fried **CHICKPEAS**?

A If you eat too many you will falafel!

Q What should you think when a boy throws a milk **CHOCOLATE BAR** at you?

A How dairy!

Q What do you get when you put **COLA** in the oven?

A Baking soda!

Q What was left after an explosion at the French **DAIRY**?

A Nothing but de-Brie!

Q Why couldn't the teddy bear finish his **DESSERT**?

A Because he was stuffed!

Q Why did the **DEVILED EGGS** cross the road?

A To get to the shell station!

Q What should you think if you get hit on the head with a can of **DIET COLA**?

A Thank goodness it was a soft drink!

Q What do you call a child's **DINNER**?

A Childish!

CHUCKLE!

Q Why did the bakers stop making **DONUTS**?

A Because they were bored with the hole business!

Q What did the **DOUGH** say to the rolling pin after receiving a compliment?

A "You flatter me!"

HAW-HAW!

Q Why should you tell everyone about the benefits of **DRIED FRUIT**?

A It's all about raisin awareness!

Q Did you hear about the gravy that stole the **DUCK SAUCE**?

A It was very sauce-picious!

Q Did you hear about the criminal **DUMPLING**?

A It showed a wonton disregard for the law!

Q What did one **EASTER EGG** say to the other?

A "Heard any good yolks recently?"

Q Did you hear about the **ÉCLAIR** that got rich and is now rolling in dough?

A No bun intended!

GIGGLE!

Q Why does **EDAM CHEESE** have such a unique taste?

A Because it's made backward!

Q What did the **EDAMAME** say to the pinto?

A "How have you bean?"

Q What do you call an **EGG** that goes on safari?

A An egg-splorer!

E

Q What did the **EGG FRIED RICE** say to the shrimp?

A "Don't wok away from me!"

Q What do French poodles and **EGG NOODLES** have in common?

A Oodles!

Q How do you make an **EGG ROLL**?

A Push it!

Q When is it hard to drink **EGGNOG** through a straw?

A When it's egg-stra thick!

Q What did the **EGGPLANT** say to the DJ?

A "Lettuce turnip the beet!"

Q Why don't **EGGS** tell each other jokes?

A They'd crack each other up!

GUFFAW!

Q Why is **EGGS BENEDICT** the perfect breakfast?

A Because it is beyond re-poach!

Q What happens when **ENGLISH MUFFINS** fight?

A They both get buttered!

Q Why doesn't the hamburger stand serve **ESCARGOT**?

A Snails are not fast food and nobody's got slime for that!

Q Why does **ESPRESSO** taste like mud?

A Because it was ground a couple of minutes ago!

20

Q What do you call a **FILLET STEAK** wearing a monocle and a three-piece suit?

A Sir Loin!

Q How do you tuna **FISH**?

A Adjust its scales!

Q When you look at **FISH STICKS**, what do you see?

A You seafood!

Q Have you seen the movie about **FLAPJACKS**?

A Don't bother, it was critically panned!

Q How do you know when people love your curry and **FLATBREAD**?

A When there is naan left!

HAH!

F

Q What type of **FLOUR** do dolphin bakers use?

A All-porpoise flour!

Q What is a robot's favorite **FOOD**?

A Microchips!

Q Did you know that **FRENCH FRIES** are not made in France?

A They are actually made in grease!

Q Why am I afraid of **FRENCH PASTRY CHEFS**?

A They give me the crepes!

CACKLE!

Q Why did the drummer order **FRIED CHICKEN**?

A Because he needed new drumsticks!

Q Where can you find the best tasting **FRITTER**?

A At a corn-ival!

Q Why was the **FROZEN YOGURT**
so bad at tennis?

A It had a soft serve!

Q If **FRUIT** comes from a fruit tree, where do eggs come from?

A A poul-tree!

Q Why is a **FRUITCAKE** like a history lesson?

A It's full of dates!

TEE-HEE!

Q Why did the **FUNGUS** have to pay for two tickets on the bus?

A Because it took up too mushroom!

23

Q How many vampires showed up to the **GARLIC-EATING** competition?

A Countless!

Q What's the best day to eat **GELATO**?

A Sundae!

Q Have you heard the joke about the **GERMAN SAUSAGE**?

A It's the wurst!

Q How did the **GINGERBREAD MAN** heal his injured leg?

A By icing it!

Q Why is **GORGONZOLA CHEESE** always sad?

A Because it's blue!

CHORTLE!

Q Why didn't the **GOUDA CHEESE** want to get sliced?

A It had grater plans!

Q What happens if you stand in the pouring **GRAIN**?

A You get all wheat!

Q Why does no one make jokes about **GRAINS**?

A They're so corny that people can barley stand hearing them!

Q What did the green **GRAPE** say to the purple grape?

A "Stop holding your breath!"

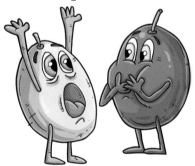

Q Did you hear about the comedian who drank a pot of **GRAVY**?

A She was a laughingstock!

HAHAHA!

25

Q What do you get when you burst a balloon filled with **GREEK YOGURT**?

A Pop culture!

HA HA!

Q What acting job did the **GREEN BEAN** audition for?

A The casserole!

Q What type of **GREEN VEGETABLES** do librarians like?

A Quiet peas!

Q What is **GUACAMOLE'S** favorite type of exercise?

A Avo-cardio!

Q Why do trains like **GUM** so much?

A Because they chew-chew!

Q Where do **HAMBURGERS** go to dance?

A The meatball!

Q Why did the astronomer use two **HAMS** to row her boat?

A She liked meaty-oars!

Q What's it called when **HASH BROWNS** play tag?

A Hashtag!

Q Would you like to hear a joke about **HAZELNUT SPREAD**?

A Sorry, I'm nutella-n you!

Q Did you hear the joke about the **HERBS** and the fish?

A I'll tell you later, this isn't the thyme or the plaice!

Q What's the opposite of **HIMALAYAN SALT**?

A Herastandin pepper!

Q Why was the **HONEY** container always open?

A Because it was a jar!

Q What do you call a **HONEYDEW** that is upset?

A Melon-choly!

Q How do you truly enjoy a **HOT DOG**?

A With relish!

Q What is a frog's favorite **HOT DRINK**?

A Hot croak-o!

HA HA!

28

Q What's an electrician's favorite **ICE CREAM** flavor?

A Shock-a-lot!

Q What did the **ICE CUBE** say to the glass of water?

A "I'm cooler than you!"

Q What's the difference between a unicorn and a head of **ICEBERG LETTUCE**?

A One is a funny beast, and the other is a bunny feast!

Q Why shouldn't you use **"IRISH_STEW"** as a password?

A Because it's not stroganoff!

Q Why did the doctor refuse to treat the **ITALIAN SAUSAGE**?

A It was already cured!

LOL!

Q What do you call an inexpensive smoked **JALAPEÑO**?

A A cheap-otle!

Q Why should you never gossip about **JAM**?

A Someone is bound to spread it!

SNICKER!

Q Why did the chef want to create a unique **JELLY**?

A To preserve her legacy!

Q Why did the **JELLY BEANS** go to college?

A They wanted to be smarties!

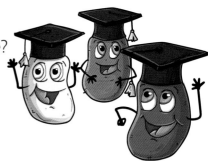

Q Why did the fruit turn itself into **JUICE**?

A Because of pear pressure!

Q Why is **KALE** never lonely?

A Because it comes in bunches!

HE HE!

Q What do you call a silent **KEBAB**?

A A shh-kebab!

Q How did the police solve the case of the stolen **KETCHUP**?

A They caught the thief red-handed!

Q Why do **KEY LIMES** make excellent actors?

A Because they are citric-ally acclaimed!

Q How do **KIWI FRUIT** get to know each other?

A They ask, "Kiwi be friends?"

L

Q What's the difference between a **LAMB DISH** and a slow computer?

A One is a rack of lamb, the other is a lack of ram!

Q Why is **LASAGNA** such an easy dish to make?

A It's a pizza cake!

Q What medicine do you give a sick **LEMON**?

A Lemon-aid!

Q Why does **LEMON MERINGUE PIE** cost $5 in Cuba and $3 in Jamaica?

A Those are the pie-rates of the Caribbean!

GIGGLE!

Q Which baseball player had the **LEMONADE**?

A The pitcher!

Q What is a kayaker's favorite kind of **LETTUCE**?

A Row-maine!

Q What do you get when you cross a cat with a **LIME**?

A A sourpuss!

Q Why was the **LOAF** in a cage at the zoo?

A Because it was bread in captivity!

Q What do you get when you cross **LOBSTER BISQUE** and a Cadillac?

A A souped-up car!

Q Which friends do you always take to **LUNCH**?

A Your tastebuds!

HA HA!

33

Q What do you call a **MAC 'N' CHEESE** that's standing right next to you?

A Too-close-for-comfort food!

CHUCKLE!

Q What kind of parents name their child **MACADAMIA**?

A A couple of nuts!

Q What do you call fake **MACARONI**?

A Im-pasta!

Q Why did the **MANGO** stop rolling down the hill?

A It ran out of juice!

Q Why is **MAPLE SYRUP** always so tearful?

A Because it's sappy!

Q What would happen if we got rid of all the **MARGARINE**?

A The world would be a butter place!

Q What did one jar of **MARMALADE** say to the other?

A "Orange you glad to see me?"

Q What happens when you dream of eating a giant **MARSHMALLOW**?

A When you wake up, you can't find your pillow!

Q What did the **MAYONNAISE** say when someone opened the refrigerator door?

A "Close the door! I'm dressing!"

Q What part of a **MEAL** makes you most sleepy?

A The napkin!

TEE-HEE!

Q Why should you never open emails about canned **MEAT**?

A They're spam!

Q Why did the **MEATBALL** tell the spaghetti to go to sleep?

A It was pasta bedtime!

BWAHAHA!

Q What did one **MELON** say to the other when he lost his keys?

A "Honeydew you know where my keys are?"

Q Where do astronauts go to get **MILK**?

A The Milky Way!

Q How do you feel when you're drinking a **MILKSHAKE** on a cliff?

A Ledge-n-dairy!

Q Why did the math teacher ask her pupils to eat **MINTS**?

A To improve their menthol arithmetic!

HAH!

Q What do you find on the ground in a **MOZZARELLA** forest?

A Cheese sticks!

Q If the **MUFFIN** man lives on Drury Lane, where does the ice cream man live?

A On Rocky Road!

Q Why was the **MUSHROOM** always invited to parties?

A Because he was a real fungi!

Q Which Canadian singer really cuts the **MUSTARD**?

A Celine Dijon!

Q What did the chocolate sauce say to the **NEAPOLITAN ICE CREAM**?

A "I'm sweet on you!"

Q Did you hear the joke about the **NECTARINE**?

A It was pitiful!

Q You know what they say about **NEW YORK CHEESECAKE**?

A If you can bake it there, you can bake it anywhere!

Q What do you call a sad **NOODLE**?

A Upsetti spaghetti!

Q What did the **NUT** say when it sneezed?

A "Cashew!"

O

Q When should you stop pouring **OAT MILK** into your coffee?

A Before it is too latte!

Q How did Reese eat her **OATMEAL**?

A Witherspoon!

Q What should you do if someone puts **OLIVE OIL** in the engine of your car?

A Pour olive it out again!

Q Why were the two **OLIVES** fighting?

A They were pitted against each other!

Q Why are **OMELETTES** always enthusiastic?

A They are just so egg-citable!

HAHAHA!

Q What kind of horse does an **ONION** ride?

A A scallion!

SNICKER!

Q What do you call a possum eating bowl after bowl of **ONION SOUP**?

A A more-soup-ial!

Q What do you get if you cross a clown with an **ORANGE**?

A Peels of laughter!

Q Why did the man lose his job in the **ORANGE JUICE** factory?

A He couldn't concentrate!

Q Did you hear about the lazy **OYSTER**?

A It wouldn't move a mussel!

Q Did you hear about the angry **PANCAKE**?

A It kept flipping out!

HE HE!

Q What did the **PAPRIKA** say to the salt around Christmastime?

A "Seasonings' greetings!"

Q What kind of neighborhood is **PARMESAN CHEESE** usually found in?

A A grated community!

Q Did you hear about the **PARSNIP** detective?

A It got to the root of every case!

Q What do you get when you cross **PASTA** with a snake?

A Spaghetti that wraps itself around your fork!

Q Why was the **PASTRY CHEF** arrested?

A For baking and entering!

HAW-HAW!

Q What do you call an angry **PEA**?

A Grump-pea!

Q Why was the **PEACH** late for work?

A He had to make a pit stop!

Q What do you call a **PEANUT** wearing a space suit?

A An astro-nut!

Q Why did the fisherman put **PEANUT BUTTER** into the sea?

A To go with the jellyfish!

Q What do you get when two **PEAS** fight?

A Black-eyed peas!

Q What did the key lime pie say to the **PECAN PIE**?

A "You're nuts!"

Q Why did the **PEPPER** put a jacket on his baby?

A It was a little chili!

Q What did the **PEPPERONI** say to the cook?

A "You wanna pizza me?"

LOL!

Q Did you hear about the world's smallest **PICKLE**?

A It was no big dill!

CHORTLE!

Q Why did the **PIE CRUST** go to the dentist?

A It needed a filling!

Q What did the salad say to the **PINEAPPLE**?

A "Lettuce be friends!"

Q Why isn't **PITA BREAD** the most popular bread in the world?

A Because it's second to naan!

Q What do you call a sleeping **PIZZA**?

A A piZZZZZZZa!

Q How do you keep a rotten **PLUM TOMATO** from smelling?

A You pinch its nose!

Q Where will you find a description of **POACHED EGGS**?

A In a hen-cyclopedia!

Q What did one bag of **POPCORN** say to the other?

A "I bet you're pretty popular!"

Q What does a **POPSICLE** become when it melts?

A Sticky!

SNICKER!

Q What do you call a **PORK** thief?

A A ham-burglar!

Q What did the **PORK SAUSAGE** say when he won the race?

A "I'm a weiner!"

Q Why should you always have a bag of **POTATO CHIPS** close by?

A In queso emergency!

Q Why do **POTATOES** make good detectives?

A Because they keep their eyes peeled!

Q What is a **PRETZEL'S** favorite dance?

A The twist!

Q What do you call an island populated entirely by **PROFITEROLES**?

A Des-serted!

Q How do you fix a cracked **PUMPKIN**?

A With a pumpkin patch!

Q What happens if you play table tennis with a bad **QUAIL EGG**?

A First you ping, then it pongs!

Q What did the magical **QUARTER-POUND BURGER** say?

A Open sesame!

GUFFAW!

Q Did you hear the joke about the **QUATTRO FORMAGGIO PIZZA**?

A Never mind, it's too cheesy!

Q What did the dalmatian say after eating a **QUESADILLA**?

A "Wow, that really hit the spot!"

Q What's the best thing to put into a **QUICHE**?

A Your teeth!

Q How do you know when you are eating **RABBIT SOUP**?

A When you find a hare in it!

BWAHAHA!

Q Why are **RADISHES** so smart?

A Because they are well-red!

Q Why did the **RAISIN** go out with the prune?

A Because it couldn't find a date!

Q Did you hear about the **RAMEN NOODLES** that come without flavor packets?

A You can't buy them anymore; they're out of stock!

Q Why was the **RASPBERRY** all by itself?

A Because the banana split!

Q Why didn't the **RAVIOLI** get invited to hang out with the cool pastas?

A Because it was a little square!

CACKLE!

Q Why doesn't anyone order the **RED CURRY** at the pelican's restaurant?

A It comes with a massive bill!

Q What do you get when you cross a potato with a **RED ONION**?

A A potato with watery eyes!

Q What do you call a **RED POTATO** that is pretending to be a tomato?

A An imi-tater!

Q How much **RED VELVET CAKE** can a snake eat?

A Only a slither!

Q Why was the **RESTAURANT** named "Out of this World"?

A It was famous for its unidentified frying objects!

Q What happens if you make **RICE PUDDING** with old milk?

A It's quite off-pudding!

Q What happened to the **ROAST BEEF** that went missing?

A Nobody's herd!

Q What do you call a hen that stares at **ROMAINE LETTUCE** all day long?

A Chicken sees a salad!

Q What did the **RUBEN SANDWICH** say to the pickle?

A "You're dill-icious!"

TEE-HEE!

50

S

Q Why did the workers ask their boss for more **SALAD**?

A They felt they were due a celery increase!

Q Why was it so hard to get away from the **SALAD BAR**?

A Because it wouldn't lettuce leaf!

Q What did the tortilla chip say to the **SALSA**?

A "Chip dip hooray!"

Q What should you do if someone says you look like a pile of **SALT**?

A Take it as a condiment!

Q What is a shark's favorite **SANDWICH**?

A Peanut butter and jellyfish!

Q Why didn't anyone believe the kids who said they ate 23 pork **SANDWICHES**?

A People thought they were full of baloney!

Q What happened when a **SARDINE** showed up late to work?

A It got canned!

Q What do you call trick-or-treating **SAUSAGES**?

A Hallo–weiners!

Q What did the **SCRAMBLED EGGS** do when the light turned green?

A They egg-celerated!

HAHAHA!

Q How does the **SEAFOOD DIET** work?

A You see food and you eat it!

S

Q What happens if you trip in a **SEAFOOD RESTAURANT**?

A You pull a mussel!

Q How do you make **SHEEPS' MILK CHEESE**?

A Ewes' milk!

LOL!

Q What do you get if you cross an apple with **SHELLFISH**?

A A crab apple!

Q What happens if you eat a **SHEPHERD'S PIE**?

A The shepherd has to find something else to eat!

Q What did the **SHRIMP** say when it was fired?

A "This scampi happening to me!"

Q Why was the fly dancing on the top of the **SODA BOTTLE**?

A Because it said "Twist to open!"

Q Where can you mail a loaf of **SODA BREAD**?

A At the toast office!

Q How do you turn **SOUP** into gold?

A Put 24 carrots in it!

Q What did the **SPAGHETTI** say when it got tangled up?

A "Knot again!"

Q What do you call a person who writes reviews of herbs and **SPICES**?

A A seasoned expert!

HAH!

54

Q Why does the **SPINACH** need a cell phone?

A In case onion rings!

Q What did the papaya say to the **STAR FRUIT** who wouldn't stop talking?

A "You guava me a headache!"

Q What do you call a **STEAK** that falls off the barbecue?

A Ground beef!

Q What do you call a chef that will only **STIR-FRY** food?

A A wok-aholic!

Q Did you hear about the kids who invested in beef, pork and chicken **STOCK**?

A They hope to be bouillon-aires someday!

HE HE!

Q What do you call a **STRAWBERRY** that plays the trumpet?

A Tooty-fruity!

Q When do **STRING BEANS** make you feel sick?

A When they tie your stomach in knots!

Q What should you do if you forget the **SUGAR** joke?

A Sift through your mind to find it!

GIGGLE!

Q What did **SUSHI** A say to Sushi B?

A "Wasabi!"

Q What did the **SWEET POTATO** say to the pumpkin?

A "I yam what I am!"

Q Where are the best **TACOS** served?

A In the gulp of Mexico!

Q Why did the chef photograph the **TAGLIATELLE**?

A He wanted to record it for pasta-terity!

Q What did the **TANGERINE** say to its grandchildren?

A "Orange you cute!"

Q Which type of **TEA** is unavailable in space?

A Gravi-tea!

Q What does **THANKSGIVING DINNER** have in common with Halloween?

A Poultry-geist!

Q Have you heard about the cheap version of **THOUSAND ISLAND DRESSING**?

A It's hundred island dressing!

Q What do cars spread on their **TOAST**?

A Traffic jam!

Q How do you make a **TOASTED BAGEL** smile?

A Butter him up!

Q Why did the **TOFU** cross the road?

A To prove it wasn't chicken!

Q Why did the **TOMATO** turn red?

A Because it saw the salad dressing!

CACKLE!

Q What do dragons eat with their **TOMATO SOUP**?

A Firecrackers!

Q What did the teacher say to the **TORTELLINI** after the exam?

A "You pasta the test!"

Q What did the upset **TORTILLA CHIP** say?

A "I don't wanna taco about it!"

Q Who wrote the book "Making a better **TUNA FISH** sandwich"?

A May O'Nase!

Q Why did the police arrest the **TURKEY**?

A They suspected fowl play!

Q What did the **UDON NOODLES** say to the soup?

A "You make miso happy!"

BWAHAHA!

Q What do you get if you eat an entire **UPSIDE-DOWN CAKE**?

A A stomach-cake!

Q What do you call a round, green **VEGETABLE** that breaks out of prison?

A An esca-pea!

Q What is it called when a meat eater orders a **VEGGIE** sandwich?

A A missed-steak!

Q What did the salad say when the **VINEGAR** was being rude?

A "I don't like the way you're addressing me!"

Q What did the **WAFFLE** say to the waffle iron?

A "Catch you on the flip side!"

Q How do you make a **WALNUT** laugh?

A Crack it up!

Q Why didn't the pan of **WATER** laugh at the jokes in this book?

A It wasn't a fan of dry humor!

Q Why do **WATERMELONS** always have huge weddings?

A Because they cantaloupe!

Q Why was the **WEDDING CAKE** so sad?

A It was in tiers!

Q Why is it hard to photograph a field of **WHEAT**?

A It always comes out grainy!

Q How does a cat make **WHIPPED CREAM**?

A With its whiskers!

Q How do you turn **WHITE CHOCOLATE** into dark chocolate?

A Turn the lights off!

Q How much does a ship full of **WHOLE GRAIN BREAD** weigh?

A A crew-ton!

Q How do you tame **WILD RICE**?

A With a tiny saddle!

CHORTLE!

Q What should you do if your **XMAS CAKE** goes missing?

A Report it as stollen!

Q Why can't you get angry at a **YAM**?

A Because they're such sweet potatoes!

HAHAHA!

Q What did the **YEAST** say to the bag of flour?

A "I loaf you dough much!"

Q Why are **YOGURT** eaters sophisticated?

A Because they're well-cultured!

Q What is a **ZUCCHINI'S** favorite sport?

A Squash!

BWAHAHA!

LOL!

CACKLE!

HE HE!

HA HA!

First American Edition 2021
Kane Miller, A Division of EDC Publishing
Copyright © Green Android Ltd 2020
Illustrated by Vasco Icuza

For information contact:
Kane Miller, A Division of EDC Publishing
5402 S 122nd E Ave
Tulsa, OK 74146
www.kanemiller.com
www.myubam.com

Library of Congress Control Number: 2020936353

Printed and bound in Malaysia, May 2021
ISBN: 978-1-68464-209-0